CHILDREN'S LIT.
ZASLAVSKY

Tic tac toe

| DATE DUE | | | |
|---|---|---|---|
| | | | |
| | | | |
| | | | |
| | | | |
| | | | |
| | | | |
| | | | |
| | | | |
| | | | |
| | | | |
| | | | |

# TIC TAC TOE

*Also by Claudia Zaslavsky*
Count on Your Fingers African Style

# TIC TAC TOE

and other three-in-a-row games
from ancient Egypt to the modern computer

by Claudia Zaslavsky
illustrated by Anthony Kramer

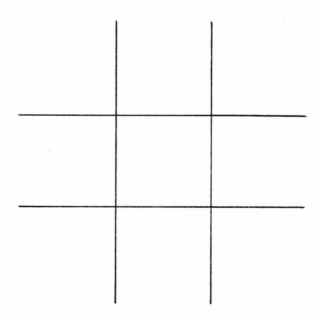

Thomas Y. Crowell New York

Text copyright © 1982 by Claudia Zaslavsky
Illustrations copyright © 1982 by Anthony Kramer

Library of Congress Cataloging in Publication Data

Zaslavsky, Claudia.
Tic tac toe.
Summary: Traces the history and development of the
three-in-a-row game for two players, popular all over
the world, that is similar to games played in ancient Egypt.
1. Tic-tac-toe—Juvenile literature.
[1. Tic-tac-toe. 2. Games] I. Kramer, Anthony, ill. II. Title.
GV1507.T47Z37 1982          794.2          82-45186
ISBN 0-690-04316-3 AACR2
ISBN 0-690-04317-1 (lib. bdg.)

1 2 3 4 5 6 7 8 9 10
First Edition

# Contents

# What This Book Is About

All over the world children play a three-in-a-row game for two players that, in the United States, is called tic-tac-toe. The game has other names. In England it is called Noughts and Crosses, in Austria it is Ecke Mecke Stecke, and in Sweden it is Tripp Trapp Trull.

Tic-tac-toe is a simple game. The 19th-century American author Mark Twain has Tom Sawyer saying, "It's as simple as tit-tat-toe, three-in-a-row, and as easy as playing hooky. I should hope we can find a way that's a little more complicated, Huck Finn."

Tic-tac-toe is one of the simplest and most recent forms of the three-in-a-row games that are popular from Iceland to the southern tip of Africa. These games of skill may be played on beautifully crafted game boards, or on diagrams traced in the earth. And they have been around for a very long time.

Who invented these games? What were the rules? Where were the games played? Why have they been popular all over the world, in all periods of history? What is their future? These are some of the questions this book will try to answer.

# About the Games

The object of most of the games in this book is to get three in a row. You will also find a three-in-a-corner game, and some in which the numbers on a line of three counters add up to a certain sum.

All of the games are for two players or two teams. You can also play them by yourself. Pretend that you are two people, and play on both sides of the board. This is a good way to learn a new game, or to work out the fine points of strategy, as though you were solving a puzzle.

Most of the games call for two kinds of counters or markers. Kings and princes used to play with beautiful pieces made of gold and ivory. Ordinary people used stones or seeds, or peeled and unpeeled twigs. You can also use red and black checkers or two kinds of coins, or make your own special counters.

The games require several types of game boards. Although you can draw them on paper, you will probably want boards that will last for a while. Use squares of mat board or styrofoam, and draw the lines neatly with a ruler. It's a good idea to make a pattern on a sheet of scratch paper first. Be sure you measure carefully.

Several shops are offering beautifully carved wooden boards, now that people are becoming more interested in three-in-a-row games.

3

Some people play games just to win, and get upset when they lose. Playing a game should be fun. When one player always wins, the other player must always lose, and may give up after a while. Helping an opponent to improve his or her skill makes the game more interesting for both players.

Each player should have an equal chance of winning. In some games the first player to move is more likely to win. Players should take turns going first in this type of game.

You may want to vary the games. A slight change in the rules, or in the shape of the game board, or in the number of counters may call for an entirely different strategy. Just be sure that both players agree on the new rules before the game starts.

# Chapter 1
## Tic-Tac-Toe

### The First Three-in-a-Row Game

Probably no one will ever discover how or when three-in-a-row games were invented. But even without ancient game boards or written records, we can still imagine how the first three-in-a-row game came to be played.

One day a wise man of some ancient tribe drew a square in the dirt. Each corner of this magic symbol represented one of the four directions—north, south, east, west. The wise man added two lines to make four smaller squares, giving the symbol greater power. Next he made special marks on the three points on each line, for three was a sacred and mysterious number.

People soon came to believe that diagrams like this one could keep away evil spirits. Only certain leaders of the tribe were allowed to draw such magic symbols.

Later, two wise men had a wonderful idea. If they could figure out a way to foretell the future, everyone would think they were gods. They placed stones on a magic square diagram and arranged them in different ways. By sunset they had worked out a set of rules. For example, getting three stones in a row meant that the tribe's herds of cattle would prosper and increase.

For a long time the people of the tribe believed that the wise men really could foretell the future. But after a while they realized that these powerful men were no different from themselves. Soon the mystery of the "magic square" had disappeared, and everyone was playing the three-in-a-row game just for fun.

Of course, the first game might have come about in an entirely different way. It is possible that two children invented it while hunting for berries. After searching all morning, pushing aside bushes with short twigs, they sat down to rest. The girl broke her twig into four pieces and drove them into the earth to make a square. The boy had peeled the bark off his twig. When he saw the sticks standing like tiny trees, he broke his twig into five small pieces. Then he pushed them into the earth, one between each pair of the girl's sticks, and one in the middle.

The girl noticed the pretty pattern made by the three rows of dark and light sticks, and had an idea. They could take turns putting their sticks into the nine holes in the ground, to see what pattern would come out. Soon they were racing, each trying to get the sticks into the ground faster.

The next day they played the game again. This time the boy had an idea that they should try to get three twigs of the same color in one row. They showed their friends, and soon everyone was playing. Years later they taught the game to their children, and they in turn taught their children. Over the years, the rules of the game changed. That's how other kinds of three-in-a-row games were invented.

Today the most popular form is tic-tac-toe.

## How to Play Tic-Tac-Toe

GAME BOARD: Draw this diagram

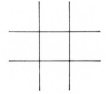

**Tic-tac-toe diagram**

on a piece of paper.

START: Toss a coin, or decide in some other way who will make the first move. The players should take turns going first, because the first to go has a much better chance of winning. Player One uses the mark X. Player Two uses the mark O.

HOW TO PLAY: Player One writes X in any of the nine spaces on the game board. Then Player Two marks O in an empty space. The players take turns placing their marks in the spaces.

OBJECT: Each player tries to get three of his or her marks in a line —across, or up and down, or along a diagonal. This line of three marks is called a row. There are only eight different ways of making a row. They are:

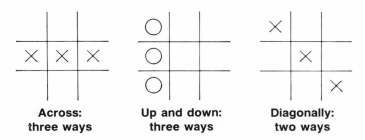

**Across:**
**three ways**

**Up and down:**
**three ways**

**Diagonally:**
**two ways**

FINISH: The winner is the first player to get three in a row. If neither player can make a row, the game is called a draw, or a tied game.

## Sample Game

This is how a game might be played. Player One uses X. Player Two uses O.

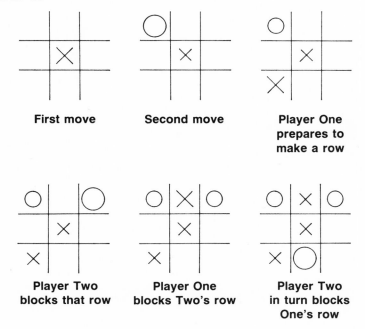

**First move**

**Second move**

**Player One prepares to make a row**

**Player Two blocks that row**

**Player One blocks Two's row**

**Player Two in turn blocks One's row**

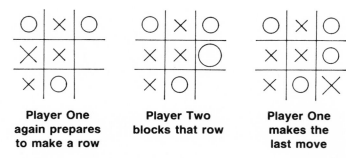

| Player One again prepares to make a row | Player Two blocks that row | Player One makes the last move |

Nobody won. This game ended in a draw.

## Try This Game

Below is the beginning of another game. Copy the diagram on your own sheet of paper. Play with a friend, or pretend that you are two players taking turns, and finish the game.

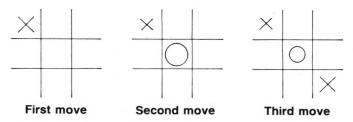

| First move | Second move | Third move |

There are many different ways to finish the game. This is one way. Player One is the winner.

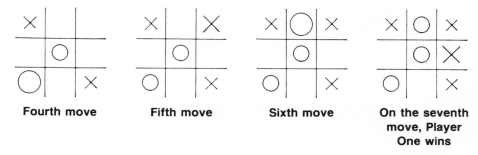

| Fourth move | Fifth move | Sixth move | On the seventh move, Player One wins |

Here is another way. This game ends in a draw.

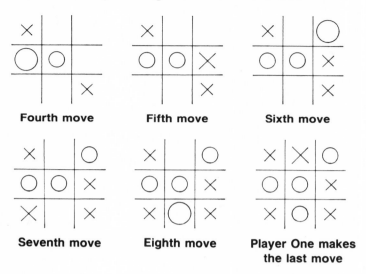

**Fourth move**   **Fifth move**   **Sixth move**

**Seventh move**   **Eighth move**   **Player One makes
the last move**

## The Finish

Half the fun of winning at tic-tac-toe is the ditty shouted by the winner.

In England it might be:

> "Tit-tat-toe,
> Here I go,
> Three jolly butcher boys
> All in a row!"

Dutch children shout:

> "Butter, milk, and cheese,
> I am the boss!"

In Sweden the winner calls out:

11

"Tripp, trapp, trull,
My mill is full!"

Very often these verses have something to do with food. Notice how the English verse mentions "butcher boys," the Dutch verse contains the words "butter, milk and cheese," and the Swedish verse refers to a "mill," a place where flour for bread is made. Children may have hoped that success in tic-tac-toe meant they would have enough to eat that night.

When the game ends in a draw, children in the United States may say, "It's a tie, cat's eye!"


## How to Be a Good Player

The players can place their X's and O's on the tic-tac-toe game board in exactly 362,880 different ways. How many of these games can be won by Player One, the first to go? How many can Player Two win? Figuring this out seems like an impossible job. Actually, it is not as hard as it seems.

Think about the two opening moves. Player One can place an X in any of nine spaces. Then Player Two can go in any of the eight remaining spaces. It appears that there are 9 times 8, or 72, possible combinations.

In fact, there are only 12, not 72, different openings. Compare the two opening moves on these four game boards. They are really all the same.

To prove that they are the same, make a model. On a blank sheet of paper draw this setup quite large, using a dark marker:

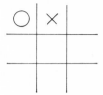

Then turn the paper. The two marks lie in four different positions:

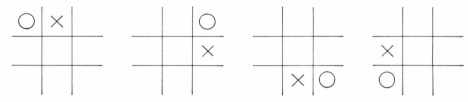

Flip the sheet of paper over to the other side, and hold it up to the light. As you turn it, you see four more positions of O and X:

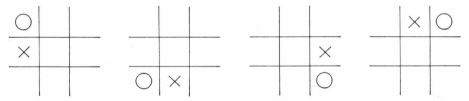

You can start with any one of the eight positions. By turning or flipping the paper, you get the other seven positions. When you examine games that start this way you are taking care of all eight positions.

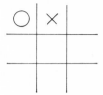

OPENING MOVES: There are actually just three different starting positions for the first player's X:

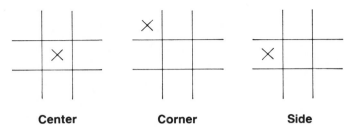

**Center**          **Corner**          **Side**

For X in the center, there are two different positions for O:

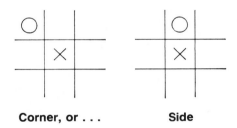

**Corner, or . . .**          **Side**

For X in a corner, there are five different positions for O:

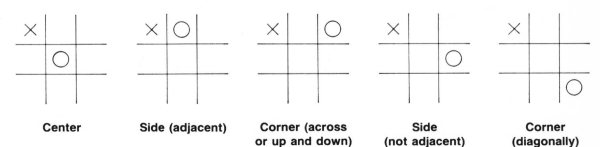

**Center**   **Side (adjacent)**   **Corner (across or up and down)**   **Side (not adjacent)**   **Corner (diagonally)**

For X on a side, there are also five different positions for O:

14

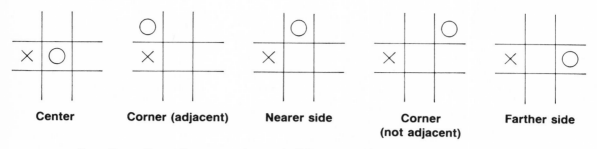

| Center | Corner (adjacent) | Nearer side | Corner (not adjacent) | Farther side |

So, altogether, there are just 12 different pairs of opening moves.

SETTING A TRAP: Player One can plan his or her second move so that Player Two is forced to go in a particular space. Then, on his or her third move (fifth move in the game), Player One tries to set up two possible ways of getting a row. This is called a trap, because Player Two can block only one of those rows, and Player One automatically wins.

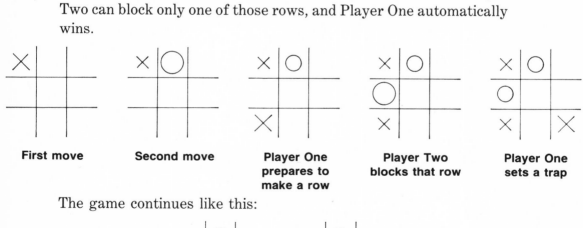

| First move | Second move | Player One prepares to make a row | Player Two blocks that row | Player One sets a trap |

The game continues like this:

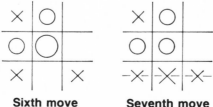

| Sixth move | Seventh move |

Or like this:

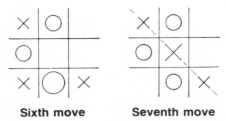

**Sixth move**          **Seventh move**

Either way, Player One is the winner.

Player One can use this "trap" strategy to win games that start in these ways:

**Player One: center
Player Two: any side**

  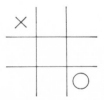 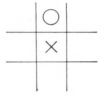

**Player One: corner   Player Two: any side or corner**

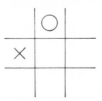 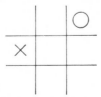

**Player One: side          Player Two:
                            nearer side
                            or farther corner**

Of the 12 possible openings, seven may end in a win for the first player. The other five will usually end in a tie. The second player can win only when Player One is careless or makes a mistake.

## Sample Games

Player One should be able to win each of these games by setting a trap. Copy each game and try to complete it.

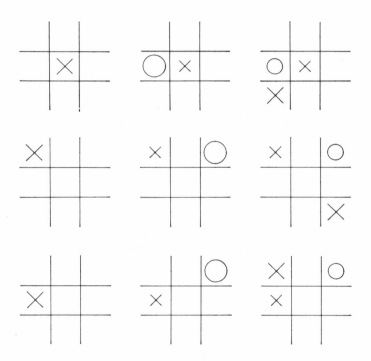

If you go first, you probably won't lose. If you go second, you probably won't win. For tic-tac-toe to be a fair game, the players should take turns going first, after the first game has been played.

## Changing the Rules

After you have figured out all the good moves, tic-tac-toe can be rather boring. Here are some other ways to play the game.

Rule that neither player may make the first move in the center.

Play eight-move tic-tac-toe. Each player makes exactly four moves, and gets a point for each row he or she makes.

Play reverse tic-tac-toe. After each player has made two moves, Player One switches to playing O and Player Two takes X.

Play toe-tac-tic. The first player to make a row is the *loser*.

Play coin tic-tac-toe. Player One has five coins of one kind, and Player Two has five coins of a different kind. The players place the coins in the small squares of the game board, instead of marking X's and O's. This game is really just plain tic-tac-toe—it only looks different.

## NUMBER TIC-TAC-TOE

COUNTERS: Nine counters numbered from 1 to 9.

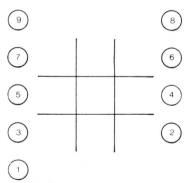

**Counters and diagram for number tic-tac-toe**

The first player takes the five odd-numbered counters: 1, 3, 5, 7, 9.

The second player takes the four even-numbered counters: 2, 4, 6, 8.

GAME BOARD: Same as for tic-tac-toe.

HOW TO PLAY: The players take turns placing a counter on the game board. All nine counters are used.

OBJECT: To make a row of three counters in which the sum of the numbers is 15. A row may contain both odd and even numbers. A player scores a point for each row he or she makes. A player can sometimes make two or even three rows in one move.

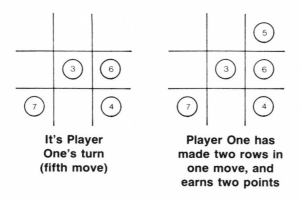

It's Player
One's turn
(fifth move)

Player One has
made two rows in
one move, and
earns two points

FINISH: The player with more points is the winner.

TAKING TURNS: For the next game, the players exchange counters.

## MAGIC SQUARE TIC-TAC-TOE

Some people believe that a certain arrangement of numbers on a tic-tac-toe diagram can bring good luck. Every line of three numbers has the same sum. This arrangement is called a magic square.

It is said that a Chinese emperor was the first person to see a magic square. Over 4,000 years ago a large turtle swam close to his

ship. The pattern on the turtle's back was a

**A Chinese magic square, with knots in black and white cord
showing the numbers**

wonderful arrangement of numbers. Every row, every column, and
each diagonal added up to 15. No wonder the Chinese thought it was
magic. In time, people all over the world were making magic
squares.

Here's how to play magic square tic-tac-toe:

COUNTERS: Nine counters numbered from 1 to 9.

GAME BOARD: A square divided into three rows and three columns.

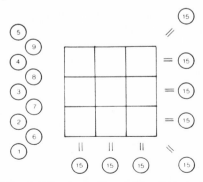

**Counters and diagram for magic square tic-tac-toe**

21

OBJECT: To arrange the nine counters so that each row, each column, and each diagonal has a sum of 15, eight sums in all. You can play this game by yourself, or take turns with a partner and cooperate to make a magic square. Each player may place any one of the nine counters on the game diagram.

HINTS: Complete the magic squares below. Then try to arrange the counters to make other magic squares. There are eight altogether.

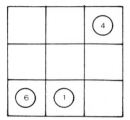 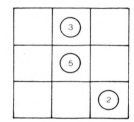

# Chapter 2

# Nine Holes,
# Three Men's Morris,
# and Similar Games

Long before anyone had heard of tic-tac-toe, people were playing Nine Holes. It was a favorite among the boys who herded sheep and cattle. While the animals were feeding in the pastures, two boys would dig three rows of holes, three holes in each row. They would gather three stones of one kind and three of another, and be ready to play.

The 17th-century English poet Michael Drayton described them:

> . . . The unhappy wags, which let their cattle stray,
> At Nine Holes on the heath whilst they together play.

Some of these "unhappy wags" invented strange rules for the game. On the Salisbury Plain, in southern England, the counters were not stones, but wooden pegs stuck into the earth. The players had to get down on the ground and pull out the pegs with their teeth!

In many old English churches there are sets of holes or lines for three-in-a-row games. The few boys who went to school in England centuries ago usually attended church schools. The dreary lessons

seemed to go on forever, and the boys were often tempted to sneak in a quick game of Nine Holes.

Even grown-ups were guilty of playing games when they should have been attending to the Sunday sermon. An English court record for the year 1699 tells of two men who were punished for playing Nine Holes during church services.

The religious beliefs of the New England colonists did not permit gambling or games played with dice or cards. Children who spent time in play of any kind were warned, "Satan finds some mischief still for idle hands to do." Still, both grown-ups and children in the New England colonies did play Nine Holes, as well as more complicated three-in-a-row games like Nine Men's Morris and Twelve Men's Morris.

## NINE HOLES

COUNTERS: Three counters for each player, of two different kinds, such as red and black checkers or two kinds of coins, buttons, or beans. One set of counters will be called "white" and the other set "black," although they may be other colors.

GAME BOARD: Draw this square diagram.

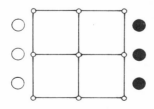

**Nine Holes diagram**

The game is played on the nine points where the lines meet.

HOW TO PLAY: Players take turns going first. Player One places a white counter on any point. Then Player Two places a black counter on any empty point. They take turns, until each player has placed all three counters on the game board. After that, the players take turns moving their counters around on the game board. On each turn, a player moves one of his or her own counters to any empty point on the board.

OBJECT: Each player tries to make a row of three counters of one color, and to block the other player from making a row. There are six different ways to make a row: three across, and three up and down.

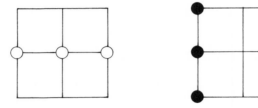

**To win at Nine Holes, a player must make a row of three across or up and down**

FINISH: The winner is the first player to make a row. If neither player makes a row, the game is a draw. The players can decide to call the game a draw at any time. If both players are careful, a game can go on for a long time.

SETTING A TRAP: In Nine Holes the players try to move their counters so that they have two different ways of making a row on their next move. This is called a trap.

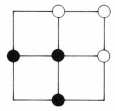

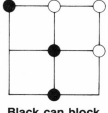

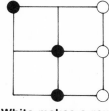

**White has set a trap**

**Black can block
only one row**

**White makes a row
and wins the game**

## Changing the Rules

As a game travels in time and space, the rules often change. The French version of this game is called Les Pendus, meaning "the hanged." In Les Pendus rows can be made along the diagonals, as well as up and down or across, eight ways in all. Player One can win easily by setting traps. For most openings the strategy is the same as for tic-tac-toe.

## How Nine Holes Became Tic-Tac-Toe

Imagine how the game of Nine Holes might have become tic-tac-toe. It could have happened in an English schoolroom. The school-master had given the students several long addition problems to work out on their slates. While the master was calling on the children on the front bench, a boy in the back nudged the student next to him. Did he have a knife to cut lines for Nine Holes in the bench? No—but why not draw the lines on the slate? They soon had a lively game going, with buttons and pebbles as playing pieces.

Suddenly they heard the master call out their names. Startled, they let all the buttons and pebbles clatter to the floor. The master gave them ten more sums as punishment for playing games in class.

The next morning one of the boys had a wonderful idea. They could make marks on the slate instead of moving pebbles and buttons. One player could mark O's (or noughts) and the other X's (or crosses). And the marks would go in the spaces, not on the points of the game board. As soon as the schoolmaster had turned his back, they tried out the new game on a board with nine spaces, like this:

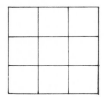

Before the end of the day, the whole class was playing Noughts and Crosses.

Soon the game had spread all over England. Some people called it tic-tac-toe, others Tip Tap Toe or Kit Cat Cannio. Tic-tac-toe became a favorite game of schoolchildren. They would draw tiny game boards in the corners of their slates. When a boy was called upon to show his work, all he had to do was to wet his finger and wipe away all the evidence. But it was not long before sharp-eared schoolmasters learned to recognize the click-clack of tic-tac-toe games going on behind their backs!

In their free time, two children would agree at the start to play a certain number of games, usually 20. At the end of each game they marked the score at the top of the slate—one point for the winner of each game. Then they erased the game board and drew a new one for the next game. A tied game was scored in the center space at the top of the slate; children called it "one for Old Nick."

In many parts of the world children play three-in-a-row games

**Tic-tac-toe played on a slate, keeping score at the top**

that have been passed down from parents to children by word of mouth and by example. The same game may be known by different names in different countries. Tapatan in the Philippines has exactly the same rules as Three Men's Morris (also called Three Penny Morris) in England, the Six Men's Game in China, Dris among the Arabs, and "the devil's game" in northern Africa. The game board may be a square, a triangle, or an octagon. Each player has three or four counters. Moves are usually made along the lines of the game diagram.

## TAPATAN

Some Philippine families keep beautiful wooden game boards for Tapatan, while others have the diagrams marked on the floors or doorsteps of their homes. They use special round counters for this game, three of light wood and three of dark wood.

COUNTERS: Three counters for each player.
GAME BOARD: Draw this diagram.

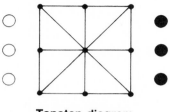

**Tapatan diagram**

The game is played on the nine points where the lines meet.

HOW TO PLAY: Players take turns going first. Player One places a white counter on any point; then Player Two places a black counter on any empty point. They take turns until all the counters have been placed on the game board. Then Player One moves one of his or her counters along a line to the next empty point. Jumping over a counter is *not allowed.* Player Two does the same with one of his or her counters, and they continue to take turns.

OBJECT: Each player tries to make a row of three counters of one color, and to block the other player from making a row. A row can be made in eight different ways: three across, three down, and two along the diagonal.

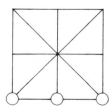 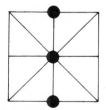 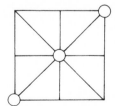

**To win at Tapatan, a player must make a row of three across,
up and down, or diagonally**

FINISH: The winner is the first player to make a row. If neither player can get three in a row, the game is called a draw. The game ends in a draw when the same set of moves has been repeated three times, and it is clear that neither player can win.

## Sample Games

The center is the best starting position for Tapatan, because four different rows go through the center. Player One is almost sure to win by placing the first counter in the center. This is how the game might go:

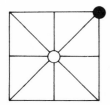

**White: center
(first move)
Black: corner
(second move)**

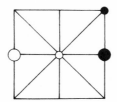

**White: side
opposite Black
Black blocks White**

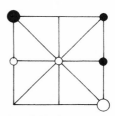

**White in turn
blocks Black
Black blocks
White again**

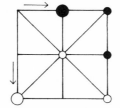

**White prepares
to make a row across
Black has a choice
of two moves**

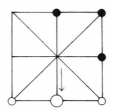

**White makes a row
and wins the game**

31

If Player One does not start in the center, Player Two should grab that spot. The game might be played like this:

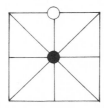

**White: side (first move)**
**Black: center (second move)**

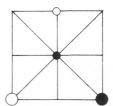

**White: corner**
**Black prepares to**
**make a diagonal row**

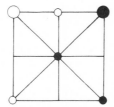

**White blocks Black's row**
**Black in turn blocks**
**White and prepares**
**to make an**
**up-and-down row**

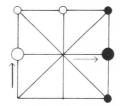

**White could make**
**any of three**
**different moves,**
**but cannot block Black**
**Black makes a row**
**and wins the game**

## Changing the Rules

Games similar to Tapatan are played in many parts of the world. Here are other versions:

Marelle (France). Neither player may make the first move in the center.

Achi (Ghana). Each player has four counters instead of three.

Tant Fant (India). The game opens with each player's three counters already in position, as shown in the diagram.

32

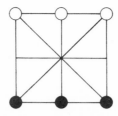

**Opening positions for players in Tant Fant**

A row may not be made on the starting lines. There are just six different ways to make a row.

## SHISIMA

Children in western Kenya play a game called Shisima, which means "a body of water." Water bugs move so quickly that it is hard to keep them in sight. The counters in Shisima are called *imbalavali*, or water bugs, because they move so rapidly around the game board.

COUNTERS: Three counters for each player.
GAME BOARD: An octagon (eight-sided polygon). To make a Shisima board, first draw a large circle and mark the center.

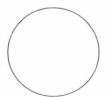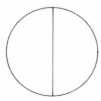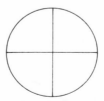

**Drawing an octagon**

Draw a line through the center—this is called a diameter. Draw another diameter, so that the two form a cross. Then draw two more diameters. Now connect the endpoints. Then draw the *shisima,* or body of water, in the center.

HOW TO PLAY: The game opens with each player's counters placed as shown in the diagram. Player One moves a white counter along a line to the next empty point; then Player Two moves a black counter one space along a line to an empty point. A player may move into the center, or *shisima,* at any time, but jumping over a counter is *not allowed.*

**Opening positions for players in Shisima**

OBJECT: Each player tries to make a row of three counters of one color. A row can be made in only four different ways, because every row has to go through the center.

FINISH: The first player to get all three *imbalavali* in a row is the winner. The game ends in a draw when the same set of moves has been repeated three times.

HINT: In this game it may not be wise to move into the center right away.

## TSORO YEMATATU

In the African country of Zimbabwe, children play Tsoro Yematatu. The name means "the stone game played with three."

34

COUNTERS: Three counters for each player, of two different kinds. Today children in Zimbabwe like to use bottle caps instead of stones.
GAME BOARD: Draw this diagram.

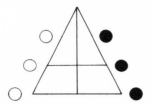

**Tsoro Yematatu diagram**

The game is played on the seven points where lines meet
HOW TO PLAY: The two players take turns placing their counters on the empty points of the board. Then each player in turn moves one of his or her counters to an empty point on the board.
OBJECT: Each player tries to make a row of three. In this game a row can be made in five different ways.
FINISH: The winner is the first to make a row. The game can go on for a long time, unless the players decide to call it a draw.


## MU TORERE

Mu Torere is a game played by Maori children in New Zealand. It is like a three-in-a-row game without actually being one. We'll call it a game of three-in-a-corner, because to win you must place three counters so that they form a "corner."
COUNTERS: Four counters for each player. We'll call one set "white" and the other "black."

**Mu Torere diagram**

GAME BOARD: The game board is an eight-pointed star. The center space is called the *putahi*. Maori children draw the diagram on the ground with a pointed stick, or on a flat rock with a piece of charcoal. The Shisima game board will do just as well.

PLACING THE COUNTERS: Counters are arranged as shown in the diagram.

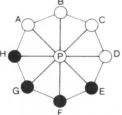

**Opening positions for players in Mu Torere; P is the *putahi***

OBJECT: To block the other player from moving.

MOVING THE COUNTERS: Black starts. Players take turns moving their counters one at a time. A move can be made in one of three ways:

1. From one point on the octagon to the next point, but only if it is empty.

2. From the *putahi* to an empty point.

3. From a point to the *putahi*, but only if the opponent occupies the point on one or both sides of that point. For example, Black can move into the *putahi* from point E or point H, but not from point F or point G.

## Changing the Rules

After each player has made two moves, any counter can be moved from a point to the *putahi*.

## How to Be a Good Player

A game between two skilled and careful players ends in a tie. A player cannot lose while his or her counter is in the *putahi*. The player who first gets three-in-a-corner with an empty point between has won the game.

**Three-in-a-corner—the winning formation for Mu Torere**

Beware of three of the other player's counters in V-formation, as in A-P-B. If Black moves from H to G,

then White moves from A to H, blocking Black, and winning the game. Black would be wise to move from F to G, forcing White out of the *putahi* on the next move.

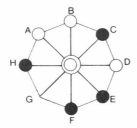

# Chapter 3

## Games on Larger Boards

Over 100 years ago, scientists examining the rooftop of an ancient Egyptian temple found several strange diagrams carved in the sandstone slabs. They could not have been religious symbols—a rooftop is no place for an important symbol. The diagrams looked like this:

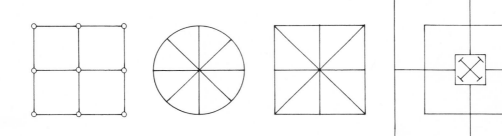

Compare these diagrams with the game boards in Chapter 2. The first must be a Nine Holes board. The second is almost the same as the Shisima board. The third is like the board for Tapatan. The last is used today for Nine Men's Morris, a game we'll learn to play in Chapter 4.

This 3,300-year-old temple to the memory of Pharaoh Seti I stands

on the west side of the Nile River. (The Egyptians believed this was where the setting sun entered the spirit world for the night.) We have learned about the pastimes of Egyptian kings and queens and other wealthy people from the paintings and writings on the walls of such temples. Game boards and carved game pieces were buried with the mummies of important Egyptians for their amusement in the "life after death." But no game boards for three-in-a-row games have been found inside the tombs. This has led historians to believe that in ancient Egypt, three-in-a-row games were played mainly by working people.

Scientists could see that parts of three diagrams had been lopped off when the great sandstone slabs were trimmed. Most likely the stonemasons played these games at the construction site during their lunch break. Instead of drawing a fresh game board in the sand for each game, they carved permanent diagrams in stone.

The Egyptians may have learned three-in-a-row games from their African ancestors. From Egypt the games could easily have spread all over the world. Greek scholars traveled to Egypt for higher education, just as people nowadays go to college. The Romans, who probably learned the games from the Greeks, spread them when they conquered Europe, the Middle East, and North Africa. By that time the Chinese had already been playing three-in-a-row games for centuries. Game diagrams were often carved on the tops of stone walls and the steps of buildings, and can still be found in many parts of the world.

A thousand years ago the Vikings struck terror in the hearts of the peoples of Europe, northern Africa, and Asia. Their swift boats enabled them to appear suddenly, and while they sometimes came to trade, they raided and invaded just as often.

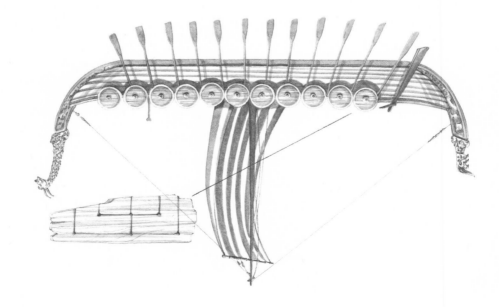

The greatest honor that could be paid to a Viking prince or merchant was to bury him in his ship, surrounded by his most precious possessions. A 1,000-year-old burial ship was unearthed a century ago at Gokstad, Norway. Among the beautiful furnishings was a wooden game board with a diagram of three connected squares. It was exactly like one of the diagrams on the roof of Seti I's temple. The ship's sailors had cut similar diagrams in the wooden planks of the deck for their own games.

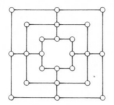

The design of a game board found on a Viking burial ship

Norwegians still use the same board today for the game they call Mølle, which means "mill." In England this game is known as Nine Men's Morris. Five Men's Morris is a simpler version of this game, using fewer counters and a smaller game board. Five Men's Morris was popular several hundred years ago in Italy, France, and England.

## FIVE MEN'S MORRIS

COUNTERS: Five counters for each player.

GAME BOARD: Copy this diagram.

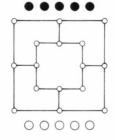

**Five Men's Morris diagram**

The game is played on the 16 points where lines intersect.

HOW TO PLAY: The two players take turns placing one counter at a time on an empty point on the board. When all ten counters have been placed, the players take turns moving one counter at a time along a line to the next empty point. Jumping over a counter is *not allowed.*

OBJECT: Each player tries to get three counters in a straight line along any side of the small or the large square. This is called a mill. A player who makes a mill at any stage of the game is allowed to

remove one of the other player's counters from the board. However, a counter may *not* be removed from the opponent's mill unless no other counter of that color is on the game board. A captured counter is not used again in that game.

FINISH: The loser is the player who has only two counters left on the board, or who is blocked from moving.

## Sample Game

Here is the beginning of a game of Five Men's Morris. Each player has placed all five counters on the board. Copy this setup on your board and complete the game, either playing with someone else or playing both sides yourself.

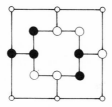

## How to Be a Good Player

Whenever possible, place your counters so that they can move in two or three directions. The black counter can move in any one of three ways. The white counter can move in only two different ways.

Position three counters so that you can shift one back and forth to "open" and "close" a mill. Every time you close a mill, you capture one of your opponent's counters.

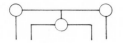

**White plans
to make a mill
on the next move**

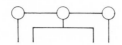

**White "closes"
the mill and captures
a black counter**

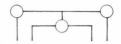

**White "opens"
the mill again, and
can close it again
on the next move**

You can defend against the "open and close" move by moving your counters onto the three points nearest the opponent's mill, as shown in the diagram. In this case, if White had only three counters left on the board, Black would win, because White would not be able to move at all.

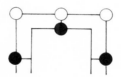

**Black has blocked White's "open and close" move**

Even better than the "open and close" move is the "shuttle" move. Position all five counters so that you can make a mill on *each* move by shifting the center counter back and forth, like a shuttle.

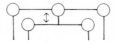
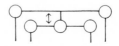

**The "shuttle" move—White makes a mill on every turn**

## Changing the Rules

Try playing Six Men's Morris. In this game, each player has six counters. Follow all the other rules for Five Men's Morris. This game is called Akidada in Nigeria.

## FIVE SQUARE

Five Square, a Chinese game, has some features of Nine Holes and some features of Five Men's Morris.

COUNTERS: Five counters for each player.

GAME BOARD: A checkerboard of five rows and five columns.

PLACING THE COUNTERS: Counters are in place on the opposite edges of the game board.

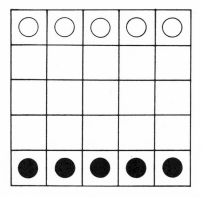

**Opening positions for players in Five Square**

MOVING THE COUNTERS: Each player in turn moves one of his or her counters one space to the next empty space. Counters may move up or down or sideways.

45

OBJECT: To make a *row* of three counters on one color, up and down or across. That player then removes one of the opponent's counters from the board. Captured counters are not used again in that game. A row may not be made on the starting lines. There are 24 different ways to make a row, so keep a watchful eye on your opponent's counters.

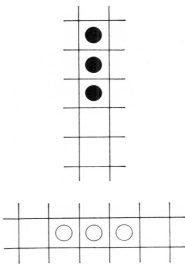

**Two ways to make a row in Five Square;**
**counters must lie in a line with no empty spaces between them**

FINISH: The winner is the first player to capture three of the opponent's counters.

The Pueblo Indians of New Mexico play three-in-a-row games similar to those found halfway around the world. Did they make up these games themselves, or did they learn them from other people? One clue is the name of the game. Some of the Pueblo people called their games Pitarilla or Picaria. These words sound like the name of the Spanish game Pedrería, which means "little stone." Most likely the Indians of the Southwest learned the games from the Spanish.

In the 16th century the Spanish conquistadores sailed from Spain to America, searching for riches. They heard about the seven towns of the Zuni people, with their tall brick buildings. The Spanish thought these must be the fabled Seven Cities of Cíbola, filled with gold! They attacked the towns, but found neither gold nor precious stones.

The Spanish conquerors gave the name Pueblo to the Zuni and other Indians of the Southwest. *Pueblo* is a Spanish word that means both "people" and "town."

The Spanish forced the Pueblo to work like slaves and to give up their own religions for Christianity. At last the Pueblo could take it no longer. In 1680 they rose against the Spanish. After a fierce struggle some of the Pueblo peoples gave in to Spanish demands. Others, like the Zuni, bravely continued to practice their traditional religions and customs.

Imagine how the Native Americans must have hated the Spanish! Yet they played games that they had learned from their conquerors.

Pueblo children scratch their game boards on flat stones or on the roofs of their adobe houses. They play with pebbles, corn, or bits of pottery.

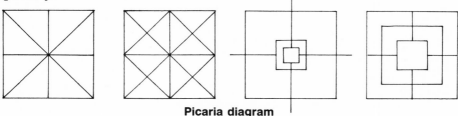

**Picaria diagram**

# PICARIA

COUNTERS: Three counters for each player, of two different kinds.
GAME BOARD: Copy this square diagram. The game is played on the nine marked points.

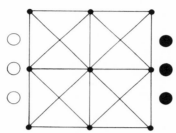

HOW TO PLAY: The two players take turns placing one counter at a time on an empty point on the board. When all six counters have been placed, the players take turns moving one counter at a time along any line to the next empty point. Jumping over a counter is *not allowed*.

OBJECT: Each player tries to make a row of three counters of the same color. A row can be made across, up and down, or diagonally. Altogether there are eight ways to win.

FINISH: The winner is the first player to make a row. If neither player can get three in a row and the game becomes boring, call it a draw.

HINTS: This game is similar to Tapatan (see Chapter 2). However, the strategies for Tapatan may not work for Picaria. Try to figure out a winning strategy.

## Changing the Rules

Some people play Picaria on the 13 points marked on this game board. Follow the rules above, but with these differences:

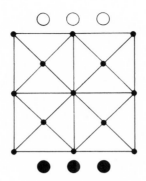

**The 13-point Picaria diagram**

1.   Neither player may place a counter in the center of the board until all six counters are on the board.

2.   You can make three in a row anywhere along a diagonal. There are 16 different ways to make a row.

Once you have mastered the basic game of Picaria, you can try using more than three counters for each player on either the nine-point or the thirteen-point game board.

# Chapter 4

## Nine Men's Morris

The first picture of children playing a three-in-a-row game appeared 700 years ago in the Spanish *Book of Games*. Two children sit on either side of a large board for Alquerque de Tres ("mill with three"), while a man standing behind each child points out the next move. These are poor people, barefoot and wearing plain clothing. The rules and winning strategy for the game are explained on another page.

Other pictures in this book show young men of the royal court playing Alquerque de Nueve ("mill with nine"), both with and without dice. The Spanish word *alquerque* comes from the Arabic name for the game. It is also the name of part of the mill used for pressing oil from olives.

Arabic-speaking Moors had come to Spain from North Africa in the eighth century. From them the Spanish people learned to play games like chess and Alquerque. Later the Spanish king Alfonso the Wise had this information written down in the *Book of Games*, "God has intended men to enjoy themselves with many games," he said in this book.

Three-in-a-row games were becoming popular all over Europe, among both rich and poor. Books with names like *The Good Friend* contained challenging problems for these games, as well as for chess. Beautiful game boards and game tables were made for the royal courts and wealthy homes. Some are now on display in museums. A 14th-century list of the objects in the 19 castles of the Duke of Berry included two tables for Mérelles, as the game was called in France. A book by the Italian writer Petrarch shows a game between two apes!

People often laid bets on who would win at three-in-a-row games. Sometimes they gambled away money that they owed in taxes to the church or to their lords. In the 15th century, the church banned these games, and 200 years later, a French king made a law to punish players of Mérelles. No wonder the French author of an 1840 *Encyclopedia of Games* complained that three-in-a-row games were no longer popular.

Three-in-a-row games are called "mill" in many European countries. In England the name is often Morris, with a number indicating the number of counters for each player. We've already talked about

Three Men's Morris and Five Men's Morris. Nine Men's Morris is another version. The word Morris may have come from "Moor," the name of the people who brought the game to Europe via Spain. Or it may be a form of the French name Mérelles, which means "counters."

Shepherds would dig lines in the earth to make game boards that were sometimes as large as a room. In his play *A Midsummer Night's Dream,* William Shakespeare described the effects of a rainstorm:

>The Nine Men's Morris is filled up with mud.

Boys would carve game diagrams on bins and stable floors. They played whenever they had a few minutes to spare from their work. Young men waiting for their carriages might chalk the lines on the flat top of a tall hat and play a quick game with pennies.

## NINE MEN'S MORRIS

COUNTERS: Nine counters for each player, of two different kinds.
GAME BOARD: Draw this square diagram.

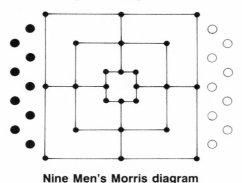

**Nine Men's Morris diagram**

The game is played on the 24 points where the lines meet.

HOW TO PLAY: The two players take turns placing one counter at a time on an empty point on the game board. When all 18 counters have been placed, the players take turns moving one counter at a time along a line to the next empty point. Jumping over a counter is *not allowed.*

OBJECT: Each player tries to make a row of three counters of the same color along any straight line. A row of three is called a mill. A player who makes a mill is allowed to remove one of the other player's counters from the board. However, a counter may *not* be removed from a mill that has been made by the opponent, unless no other counter of that color is on the board. Captured counters are not used again in that game.

 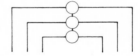

**Two ways to make a row, or mill, in Nine Men's Morris**

FINISH: The loser is the player who has only two counters left on the board, or who is blocked from moving.

## Sample Game

Here is the beginning of a game of Nine Men's Morris. All 18 counters have been placed on the board. White went first. The numbers show the order in which the white and black counters were placed. Place the counters on your board in the same order and continue the game to the end.

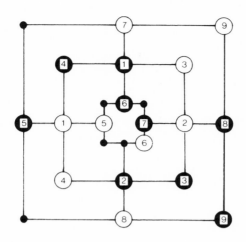

## How to Be a Good Player

When you place your counters on the board, spread them out. This makes it more difficult for your opponent to block you.

Don't try to make a mill while you are placing your counters. Make your mills during the "moving" stage of the game.

Move your counters so that you'll have a choice of more than one way to form a mill on a future move.

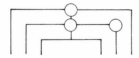

**White can make a mill in two moves, either up and down the line on which two counters are now positioned, or across the line on which two counters are now positioned**

When you place your counters on the board, try to position them so that you'll be able to move in several directions. Notice, in the diagram, that each white counter could move in any of four directions, if it was not blocked. Counters placed at corners can move in only two directions and are more easily blocked.

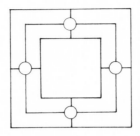

The "open and close" move works just as well in Nine Men's Morris. Place three counters so that you can shift one back and forth to "open" and "close" a mill. Every time you close a mill, you capture one of your opponent's counters.

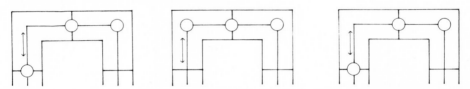

**The "open and close" move is the same as in Five Men's Morris; White can make a mill on every other turn**

Defense against the "open and close" move is the same as in Five Men's Morris. Position three counters on the three points nearest the opponent's mill, as shown in the diagram.

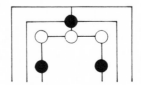

**Black has blocked White's "open and close" move**

You can also "shut out" your opponent's "open and close" move. In the example in the diagram, White is in position to open a mill. Black moves right in and "shuts out" White.

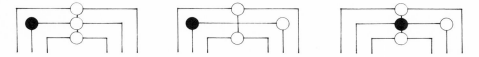

**Black "shuts out" White's "open and close" move with the effective use of just one counter**

White should have captured this black counter before it could block the mill, or else opened the mill with a different counter.

Another effective move is the "cross mill." In the diagram, the lines connecting the four counters form a cross. White can make a mill by moving any one of the four counters into the center of the cross.

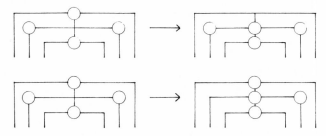

**The "cross mill"—here again White can make a mill on every other turn**

The "shuttle" move requires five counters, positioned so that by "shuttling" one of them back and forth, you can make a mill—and capture one of your opponent's counters—on every move. The "shuttle" move is also called a "running mill." If you get into this position, you should take care to capture opposing counters that threaten your position, as the black counter in the diagram does.

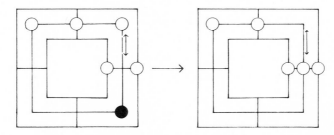

**The "shuttle" move—White makes a mill on every turn**

With six counters in "wipeout" position, as shown in the diagram, you can make a mill on every turn, and your opponent cannot threaten you. He or she will soon be "wiped out" by capture.

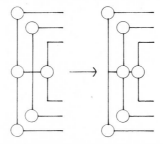

**White is in "wipeout" position—White makes a mill on every turn, and Black cannot threaten the position**

## Changing the Rules

Here are some ways to vary basic Nine Men's Morris:

Rule that a player who has only three counters left on the board may move them, one at a time, to *any* empty point on the board. This is called "hopping" or "going wild."

58

Rule that the same counter may not be moved twice in two successive turns.

Play with dice. This version of the game is described in the Spanish *Book of Games*. During the "placing" stage, the players take turns tossing three dice. If the outcome is any of these combinations:

6-5-4    6-3-3    5-2-2    4-1-1

the player captures a counter from the other player, and also places his or her own counter on the board. If this player can also make a mill, he or she can remove *two* of the opponent's counters from the board. With any other combinations of the dice, the player can place a counter on the board, and, if possible, make a mill and capture a counter from the opponent. After all the counters have been placed on the board, dice are no longer used; the game proceeds by the regular rules.

Play Trique. Children in Colombia, South America, play the game on a board in which the corners of the squares are connected by diagonal lines. Each player has nine counters. Follow the rules for Nine Men's Morris, except that moves and rows may also be made along the diagonal lines. A player who makes a row of three calls out: "Trique!" the Spanish word for a clever trick.

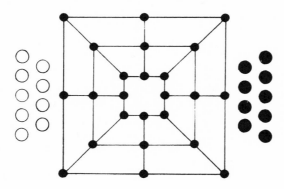

# Chapter 5
## A Dozen or So for Each Player

Very often a game dies and then comes to life again years later. People who grew up in Europe often look puzzled when they are shown a diagram for a three-in-a-row game. But after studying it for a few minutes, their faces light up. "I played that game 40 years ago!" they exclaim. "We called it Mühle in German." Or Melnitsa in Russian, or Malom in Hungarian, or Mylna in Icelandic. All these words mean "mill."

The same thing happened in the year 1826. A man in London wrote to *The Every-day Book:* "I was much pleased on reading and being reminded of an ancient game in your book, called Ninepenny-Marl, a game I had scarcely heard of during the last 20 years, although perfectly familiar to me in my boyish days." He was surprised to find that the people of his hometown were still playing this game. They called it Nine Men's Morris.

In the 19th century, information about games began to appear in magazines and books. People sent in letters about their own childhood pastimes and the customs of faraway places. Readers discovered that a game with certain rules might have many different names, while a game with a certain name might have many different sets of rules.

By that time, children were no longer thought of as small grown-ups. "Children will be children," people said. They were concerned about poor children and orphans who had to work in factories at an age when youngsters today are in elementary school. Children needed to play.

More fortunate girls and boys attended school and also had time to play. Books like *The Boy's Treasury of Sports, Pastimes, and Recreations* and *Every Boy's Book* contained descriptions and pictures of indoor and outdoor games.

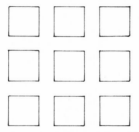

**The arrangement of chairs for the German game
of Lebende Mühle, or "living mill"**

Both girls and boys played three-in-a-row games. In the German game of Lebende Mühle ("living mill"), they became the counters. Nine chairs were arranged in three lines. Two leaders each had a team of four players and took turns seating them. If no mill, or row of three players from one team, had been formed by the time all eight players were seated, the leaders moved them from chair to chair one at a time.

English pageants featured girls and boys as counters in the game of Nine Men's Morris. Imagine the scene. In one field, knights in shining armor, mounted on prancing horses, are tilting with bared swords. In another field, men in red velvet and women in billowing

lace-trimmed gowns gather around the large Morris diagram marked in the earth. As the masters move their living game pieces along the sides of the squares, the lords and ladies call out "Good move!" or "Watch out!"

Three-in-a-row games with twelve counters for each player are the most challenging of all. The British colonists in New England enjoyed a version called Twelve Men's Morris. Playing the game helped them to bear the bitter cold on wintry evenings.

The Twelve Men's Morris board has 24 points. If the players were to have all 24 counters on the board at once, the result would be a deadlock—neither player would be able to move a counter. At least one counter must be captured during the "placing" stage of the game, leaving one or more points empty for later moves. Except for the opening, when at least one counter must be captured, Twelve Men's Morris is played just like Nine Men's Morris, as described in Chapter 4.

In the game called Nerenchi, the game board is the same as for Twelve Men's Morris, and each player has 12 counters. But the problem of how to get room to move on the board is solved in a different way.

## NERENCHI

Nerenchi is an ancient three-in-a-row game played in the Asian country of Sri Lanka. Diagrams for such games were carved in temple steps 2,000 years ago. Nerenchi has long been a special favorite of the women and girls in Sri Lanka.

COUNTERS: Twelve counters for each player or team.

GAME BOARD: Copy this diagram.

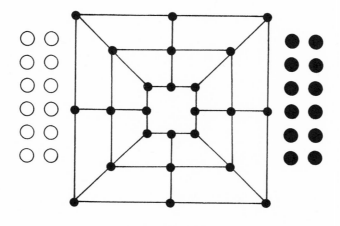

**Nerenchi diagram**
**Twelve Men's Morris diagram**

The game is played on the 24 points where lines meet.

HOW TO PLAY: The players (or teams) take turns placing one counter at a time on an empty point on the board. This part of the game ends when 22 counters are on the board, leaving two empty points. The two remaining counters are not used in the game.

The last player to place a counter on the board makes the first move. The players (or teams) take turns moving one counter at a time along a line to the next empty point. Moves may *not* be made along the diagonal lines, and jumping over a counter is not allowed.

OBJECT: Each player tries to get a row of three counters along a side of a square, along a line joining the midpoints of the sides of the squares, or along a diagonal line joining the corners. This is called a *nerenchi*. Notice that although players may not *move* along the diagonals, a diagonal *nerenchi* is allowed.

A player who makes a *nerenchi* during the "placing" stage of the game takes an extra turn, and may do so for each nerenchi. As a result, one player or team may have 12 or more counters on the board, while the other has only ten or fewer. The player who places a counter first has an advantage.

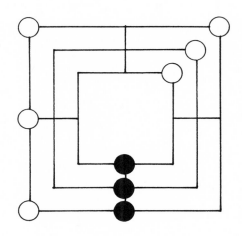

**Three ways to make a *nerenchi*;
there are 20 ways altogether**

After the "placing" stage of the game has ended, each player or team tries to make as many *nerenchi* as possible. During this part of the game, a player who makes a *nerenchi* is allowed to remove an opponent's counter from any position on the board.

FINISH: The loser is the player or team that has lost all but two counters, or is blocked from moving.

HINTS: Most of the hints and strategies for Nine Men's Morris are just as useful for Nerenchi (see Chapter 4).

## Changing the Rules

Vary Nerenchi by using exactly 11 counters apiece. Rule that a player who makes a *nerenchi* at *any time* will capture one of the opponent's counters from the board. Don't allow extra turns at the "placing" stage.

Rule that players may move counters along the diagonal lines.

Play Eleven Men's Morris by combining all of the variations in the two paragraphs above.

## MURABARABA

Until recently, boys in the southern African country of Lesotho were expected to spend their days caring for large herds of cattle. But, at the risk of punishment, they managed to get in a game of Murabaraba now and then.

Nowadays most children in Lesotho go to school during the day. And some teachers even encourage their students to play Murabaraba. A recent study showed that children who knew the game did better in their school geometry lessons than those who had never played it.

Murabaraba is no longer just a boys' pastime. Girls play, too. Often two teams play against each other, while friends gather around and shout advice. The game is so popular that the diagram for it is often marked on a large flat stone in the village square, ready for use at any time.

COUNTERS: Twelve counters for each player or team, of two different kinds.

GAME BOARD: Copy this square diagram.

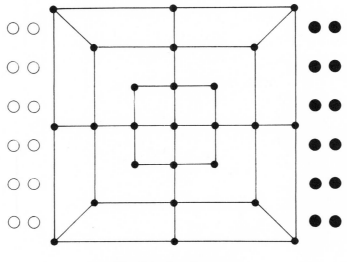

**Murabaraba diagram**

The game is played on the 25 points where lines meet.

HOW TO PLAY: The two players (or teams) take turns placing one counter at a time on an empty point on the board. This part of the game ends when all 24 counters have been placed. Then the players (or teams) take turns moving one counter at a time along any line to the next empty point. Jumping over a counter is *not allowed.*

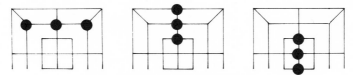

**Three different strike positions**

OBJECT: Each player tries to make a row of three counters of the same color. This is called a strike. But a line of three that ends in the center of the board is *not* a strike.

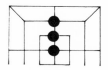

**This row of three is *not* a strike,
because it ends in the center of the game board**

A player who makes a strike may remove one of the opponent's counters from any position on the board. Captured counters are no longer used in that game.

During the "placing" stage of the game, it is possible to make two strikes at one time. When that happens, the player may capture two of the opponent's counters.

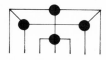 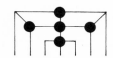

**Black is about to          And has made two
place a counter . . .          strikes in one move**

TRAPS: During the "placing" stage of the game, a player who has two counters in a row must complete the strike on the next move, if possible. This situation is called a trap. If the player can, but does not, complete his or her strike on the next turn, the opponent may remove any *two* of this player's counters from the board.

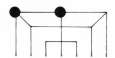 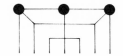

**Black is about to place a counter . . .
And must complete the strike,
or forfeit two counters to the opponent**

During the "moving" stage of the game, there are no traps. If a player's counters are blocked so that none of them may move, that player either skips a turn or gives up the game.

FINISH: The loser is the player who has only two counters left on the board, or who is blocked and gives up. A player who has only three counters on the board may "hop" them to any empty point on the board. But usually the other player has given up or lost long before this stage.

HINTS: Most of the hints and strategies for Nine Men's Morris are just as useful for Murabaraba (see Chapter 4).

## Sample Game

Set up your Murabaraba game board as shown in the diagram, and continue the game to the finish. All 24 counters have been placed on the board, and neither player has made a strike or been trapped.

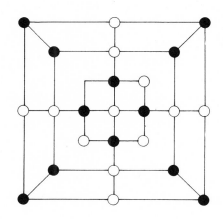

# DARA

Dara is a popular game among men and boys in Nigeria, Niger, Mali, and other parts of northwestern Africa. Good Dara players are held in great honor. After the day's work is done, champions travel from village to village, challenging local players. The contests may continue into the night for as long as the moon shines brightly.

A champion does not want his knowledge to die with him. He teaches the game to his son as soon as the child is old enough to learn the rules. Later, the father tells the boy the secrets of the game, a few at a time. These secrets often have been handed down from the champion's own father or grandfather.

COUNTERS: Twelve counters for each player.

GAME BOARD: A checkerboard of five rows, six squares in a row. In Africa they dig holes in the earth or the desert sand.

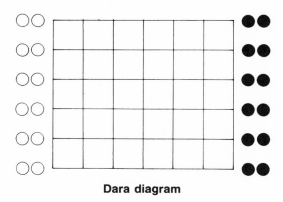

**Dara diagram**

HOW TO PLAY: The two players take turns placing one counter at a time in any empty space, until all 24 counters have been placed. Then the players take turns moving one counter at a time to the next empty space. Moves may be made up, down, or sideways, but *not*

71

diagonally. Jumping over a counter is *not allowed.*

OBJECT: Each player tries to get exactly three of his or her counters in a row, either across or up and down. When a player makes a row, he or she is allowed to remove one of the opponent's counters from the board. This is called "eating" the enemy, just as a lion eats its prey.

ADDITIONAL RULES: These rules also apply in Dara:

A player may not have more than three counters in a continuous line at any time.

A row made during the "placing" stage does not count.

A player who makes two rows in one move may capture only one of the opponent's counters.

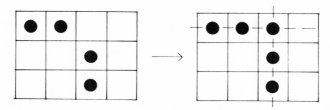

**In Dara it is possible to make two rows in one move**

A counter may never be removed from a row made by the opponent.

FINISH: The game ends when one player can no longer make a row. His or her opponent is the winner.

## How to Be a Good Player

Place your counters carefully during the first stage, so as to make as many rows as possible in the "moving" stage.

Make a "horse." Arrange five of your counters so that you can

73

shift one counter back and forth to make a row on each move. This is called a "horse"; it is a sure way to win.

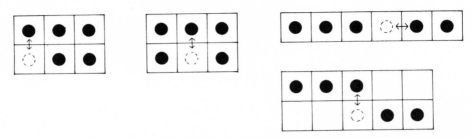

**Making a "horse," as shown, is a sure way to win at Dara**

## Changing the Rules

Some African players follow one or more of these rules for Dara:
1. Play on a checkerboard having six rows and six columns.
2. A counter may be captured from the opponent's row only if no other counter of that color is on the board.
3. Neither player may remove a counter from a row. Therefore the *"horse"* strategy cannot be used in this game. The player who makes three rows before his opponent makes one row wins the game.

## WILDEBEEST

A wildebeest is an African antelope. Although the name of this game is African, the game was actually invented by a games expert named Leon Vié. Most games have been invented by individuals, but people soon forget who they are.

COUNTERS: Eleven counters for each player, of two different kinds.
GAME BOARD: Copy this diagram.

74

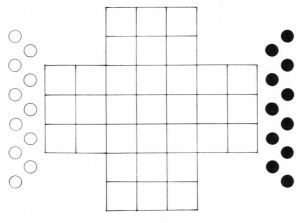

**Wildebeest diagram**

The game is played on the 33 square spaces.

HOW TO PLAY: The two players take turns placing one counter at a time on an empty square, until all 22 counters are on the board. Two counters of the same color may *not* be placed side by side. The players then take turns moving one counter to the next empty square. Counters may move up, down, or sideways, but *not* diagonally. Jumping a counter is *not allowed*.

OBJECT: Each player tries to make a "wildebeest," a row of three counters of one color. A wildebeest may be made up and down or across, but not diagonally. A player who has made a wildebeest may remove one of the opponent's counters from the board. This is called "eating" the enemy. Captured counters are not used again in that game.

FINISH: The winner is the player who has "eaten" all of the opponent's counters.

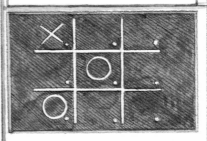

# Chapter 6

## Computers and Tic-Tac-Toe

If you should visit a computer game room, you might see a live chicken in a booth next to all the machines with their flashing lights. For a small sum of money you can play tic-tac-toe with the chicken. Chances are that you won't win the game.

A chicken is a pretty stupid bird. Can it be trained to play tic-tac-toe, to play so well that it never loses? Of course not. The chicken only seems to be playing the game. Its moves are really made by a computer.

This is how the chicken tic-tac-toe game works. The human being and the chicken play on opposite sides of a vertical tic-tac-toe game board. The board is placed so that the human can't see the chicken's side. When its turn comes, the chicken pecks at the board and gets some corn as a reward. Actually it is the computer that decides where the chicken is to move and that marks the game board. The chicken has been trained, all right, but not to play tic-tac-toe.

Having a computer play tic-tac-toe is not a new idea. As long ago as the year 1864, Charles Babbage wrote about his plans for a tic-tac-toe machine. It would show the figures of two children playing against each other. At the end of the game the winner would clap, and then the loser would cry.

Babbage was among the early inventors of the modern computer. He worked with Lady Ada Augusta Byron Lovelace, one of the first computer programmers. Unfortunately, Babbage never did build his tic-tac-toe machine.

Today you can buy a ready-made program, on a disk or a cassette, that will teach a computer how to play tic-tac-toe. Or you can get a book that lists the step-by-step instructions you can feed into a computer so that it can play the game with you. But it is more challenging to work out the instructions for yourself.

## How to Program a Computer
## to Play Tic-Tac-Toe

A smart computer will never lose a game of tic-tac-toe.

What makes a computer smart? Actually, a computer isn't smart at all. It can't come up with a good idea because it can't think. A computer will do just what it is told to do, no more and no less. However, there are some things that a computer can do better than people, because:

A computer doesn't forget. Any information that goes into the computer's memory stays there.

A computer is very fast. Some computers can carry out 80 million instructions in one second.

A computer always does as it is told. It never says, "I would rather watch TV."

A computer doesn't get tired. It can work without stopping—unless it breaks down.

The person who tells a computer what to do is called a programmer. The instructions this person gives the computer are called a program.

Imagine that you are a computer programmer. You are going to write a program for a computer to play tic-tac-toe with a human being.

You must tell the computer every detail. And you must talk to it in its own language.

Before the computer can begin to play, it must be told:

1. To print a game board that looks like this:

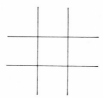

**Tic-tac-toe diagram**

2. The names of the nine small boxes. You might name the boxes after the first nine letters of the alphabet.

|   |   |   |
|---|---|---|
| a | b | c |
| d | e | f |
| g | h | i |

**Before a computer can play tic-tac-toe,
it must know the names of the nine boxes of the game board**

3. How to write its mark on the game board.
4. How to decide where to move.

Here is a simple way to instruct the computer on how to move. Tell it to place an X in box **a**, if it is empty. If not, place an X in box **b**, if that box is empty. The computer can look at each box in turn, and

79

will place an X in the first empty box. The instructions for the moves say this:

> Look at box **a**. Is it empty?   If YES, place an X in box **a**.
> If NO, go on to box **b**.
> Look at box **b**. Is it empty?   If YES, place an X in box **b**.
> If NO, go on to box **c**.

The computer continues until it has marked an X in a box.

Before writing the program, the programmer makes a step-by-step plan to be sure that all the steps are correct. This plan is called a flow chart. The flow chart below shows how the computer will make its moves. Answer each question in a diamond-shaped box with either "yes" or "no." Then follow the arrows.

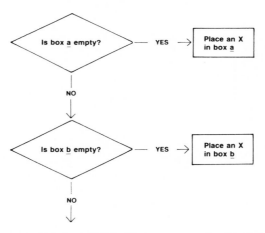

After the computer marks an X, it stops—it doesn't know what to do next. It must be told to take turns with a human, and to mark the human's moves on the game board.

The computer also needs instructions about getting three in a row, both for making its own rows and for blocking its opponent's rows.

Tell the computer to look for two X's in a row, and to place a third X in that row, if possible. If not possible, it should look for two O's in a row, and place an X in that row, thus blocking the opponent. If neither move is possible, have the computer place an X in the first empty space, as before.

A human being can find two in a row very easily, but a computer needs many instructions to carry out this job. It must look at every combination of two boxes in every one of up to eight lines until it finds two X's or two O's in a row. Then it must make sure that the third box in the line is empty before it marks an X there.

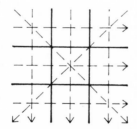

**The computer may have to look at as many as eight rows before it finds two X's or two O's in a row**

The computer must recognize when a game has ended. It needs many instructions to do this, too. When you have programmed the computer to recognize when a game is over, you can have it announce the results of each game. Program it to print:

"Nobody won this game. Would you like to play again?"
for a tied game.
"Too bad, I won," when it wins.
"Good for you. You beat me!" when it loses. The computer is not a sore loser.

81

Now try playing a game with the computer, using this program. Let the computer go first, placing an X in box **a**. Your best move is in the center as shown in Chapter 1.

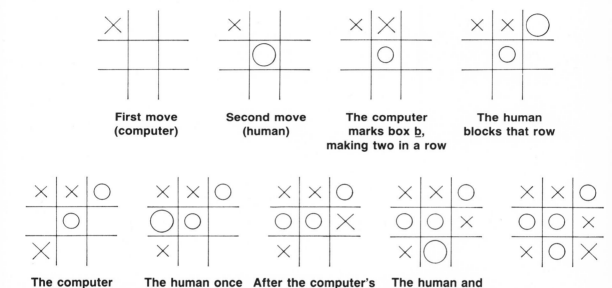

**First move (computer)**

**Second move (human)**

**The computer marks box b̲, making two in a row**

**The human blocks that row**

**The computer in turn blocks the human's row**

**The human once again blocks the computer's row**

**After the computer's fourth move, no one can make a row**

**The human and the computer fill the last two boxes**

The computer prints: "Nobody won this game. Would you like to play again?"

Accept the computer's invitation and try a different opening.

The computer prints: "Too bad, I won." It succeeded in setting a trap and winning the game.

To help the computer play an even better game, you can take advantage of its wonderful memory. Write out the instructions for the moves in many well-played tic-tac-toe games. Put all these

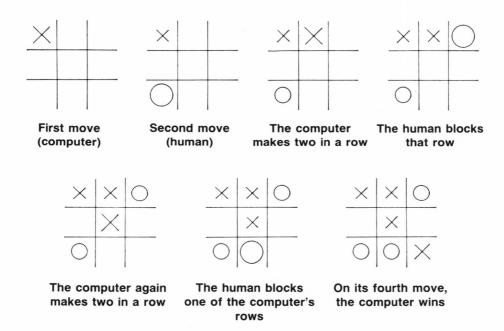

**First move
(computer)**

**Second move
(human)**

**The computer
makes two in a row**

**The human blocks
that row**

**The computer again
makes two in a row**

**The human blocks
one of the computer's
rows**

**On its fourth move,
the computer wins**

games into the computer's memory. When the computer plays a
game against a human, it can compare the moves with those in the
games in its memory, and choose the best strategy.

The computer is pretty smart.

But you are even smarter. You can program a computer to play
tic-tac-toe.

83

# Afterword

Games based on tic-tac-toe have become popular in recent years—now we have word tic-tac-toe, number tic-tac-toe, and computer tic-tac-toe. The game board has grown from a three-by-three square in two dimensions to four layers of four-by-four squares in three-dimensional space. Mathematicians analyze tic-tac-toe games that might be played on a hypercube in four-dimensional space! This shape exists only in their imagination, but that doesn't stop the mathematicians. They even go to five, six, and higher dimensions for their tic-tac-toe games—all imaginary, of course.

Psychologists have used tic-tac-toe to study the personalities of children. They have found that some young people set out to win, while more timid children only play for a draw.

No matter what your style of playing, you can have fun with three-in-a-row games. You can play a fast game without caring who wins, or you can work out a careful strategy to beat your opponent. And when you become bored, you can try a different version of the game, or make up a new one.

Wherever you might travel, you will probably find that people play some version of these games. Although you may not be able to speak their languages, you can make friends all over the world with three-in-a-row games.

# More Three-in-a-Row Games
## Played Around the World

These games have not been mentioned in the book. However, the directions for playing them are the same as for games that have already been described.

A. Follow the directions for Nine Holes (page 25):

| | |
|---|---|
| Arabic-speaking countries | Drīs ath-thalātha |
| Germany | Nulochen; Neun Löcher |
| India | Tre-guti |
| Japan | San-noku-narabe |
| Netherlands | Dreisticken |
| Nigeria | Akidada |

B. Follow the directions for Tapatan (page 30):

| | |
|---|---|
| Arabic-speaking countries | El-Qirqāt |
| France | Marelle Assise |
| Iran | Hujura |
| Ireland | Cashlan Gherra |
| Italy | Filo; Mulino |
| Spain | Tres en Raya |

C. Follow the directions for Nine Men's Morris (page 53):

| | |
|---|---|
| Arabic-speaking countries | Drīs |
| Germany | Mühle |
| Greece | Triodi |
| Hungary | Malom |
| India | Nao-guti |
| Indians of California | Yakamaido |
| Indians of Southwest U.S. | Pitarilla; Picaria; Paitariya |
| Italy | Mulinello |
| Nigeria | Akidada |
| Russia, | Melnitsa |
| Sweden | Qvarn |

D. Follow the directions for Trique (page 59), except that each player has twelve counters:

| | |
|---|---|
| Burma | Thon-htap Kya |
| China | Sam K'i |
| Korea | Kon-tjil |
| Malaysia | Dig Dig |
| Somalia | Shah |
| U.S., New England Colonies | Twelve Men's Morris |

85

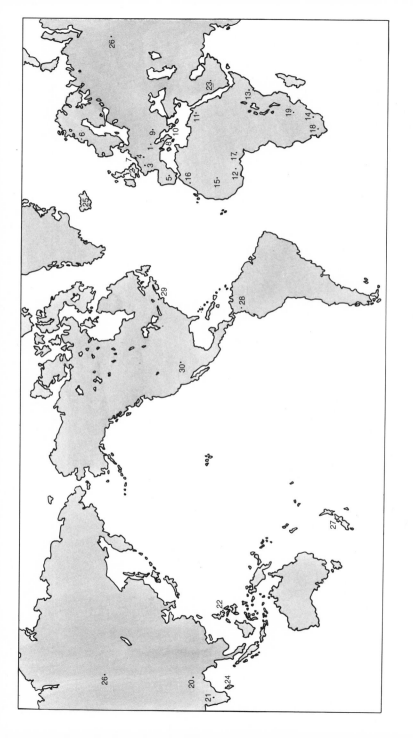

PLACES MENTIONED IN THIS BOOK

| | | | | | |
|---|---|---|---|---|---|
| 1 | Austria | 11 | Egypt | 20 | China | 25 | Iceland |
| 2 | England | 12 | Ghana | 21 | India | 26 | Russia |
| 3 | France | 13 | Kenya | 22 | Philippines | 27 | New Zealand |
| 4 | Germany | 14 | Lesotho | 23 | Saudi Arabia | 28 | Colombia |
| 5 | Spain | 15 | Mali | 24 | Sri Lanka | 29 | New England |
| 6 | Norway | 16 | Morocco | | | 30 | New Mexico |
| 7 | Netherlands | 17 | Nigeria | | | | |
| 8 | Italy | 18 | South Africa | | | | |
| 9 | Hungary | 19 | Zimbabwe | | | | |
| 10 | Greece | | | | | | |

# Index